IS-908: Emergency Management for Senior Officials

By

Fema

10/31/2013

Welcome

The purpose of this course is to introduce senior officials to the important role they play in emergency management.

The responsibility for preparing for, responding to, and recovering from incidents, both natural and manmade, begins at the local level – with individuals and public officials in the county, city, or town affected by the incident.

Course Objectives

After this course, you should be able to:

- Identify the emergency management role assumed by senior officials.
- Describe emergency management authorities.
- Identify emergency management team members.
- Describe the purpose of an emergency operations plan.
- State the importance of resource management, training, and exercises.
- Identify the role of the senior official during a crisis.
- Describe the importance of involving the whole community in preparedness.

Course Features

This course includes the following features:

Simple steps you can take to become acquainted with your emergency management role, authorities, and team members.

Video presentations sharing lessons learned from officials of the City of Baton Rouge, East Baton Rouge Parish, Louisiana.

Chief Elected or Appointed Official

A mayor, city manager, or county manager, as a jurisdiction's chief executive officer, is responsible for ensuring the public safety and welfare of the people of that jurisdiction.

Specifically, this official provides strategic guidance and resources during preparedness, response, and recovery efforts. Emergency management, including preparation and training for effective response, is a core obligation of local leaders.

Emergency Management: Role of the Senior Official Audio Transcript

NARRATOR:
As an elected official, protecting the well being of the whole community is paramount. Doing so is especially critical when disaster strikes. Maintaining the community's trust and support means being prepared to lead during a crisis.

Although this story takes place in the city of Baton Rouge, in East Baton Rouge Parish—the lessons learned apply to communities across the country.

Disasters disrupt people's lives, making them feel vulnerable and depriving them of the services they rely upon. At a time of crisis, the community turns to its local government for assurance that preparations have been made to manage the incident and that their lives will return to normal as quickly as possible, with a minimum of inconvenience. The responsibility for a favorable outcome rests with local senior elected officials.

MAYOR HOLDEN:
Whenever there is an emergency, the population expects you to step up and be a leader. Now, the question is whether or not you want to accept that role. Because when you raise that hand and take that oath of office, you know, I don't think you ever anticipate that "Wow, this other situation may happen that's going to necessitate that I do something a little more in depth than what I did in taking that oath."

NARRATOR:
Mayor Holden's leadership was tested in August 2005, when Hurricane Katrina struck Louisiana. When the levees in New Orleans collapsed, 200,000 people moved into Baton Rouge. What happened three years later with Hurricane Gustav was even worse.

JAY GRYMES:
Probably the biggest, at least in the last few years, would have to be Gustav. Certainly the most impacting tropical event for the Baton Rouge area since 1965's Betsy. We saw more damage here in Gustav than we did in Andrew, even though maybe on a national scale Andrew is a more noteworthy storm.

During a time of crisis, Mayor Holden knew that the people of Baton Rouge expected to hear from him.

MAYOR HOLDEN:
I think the people expect for you to give them guidance. People expect for you to carry out basic services like fire, police, or EMS. People expect you to deal with flooding if there's a flood there. People expect you to deal with whatever disaster that has come up in an economical way, making sure they are still able to carry on with their lives, and their businesses as much as they possibly can. But they really look to you to give them some comfort, give them advice, and also do the job to make their lives a lot easier.

Key Steps for New Officials

Knowing that newly elected or appointed senior officials are very busy, this course presents the six key steps to take for ensuring community readiness.

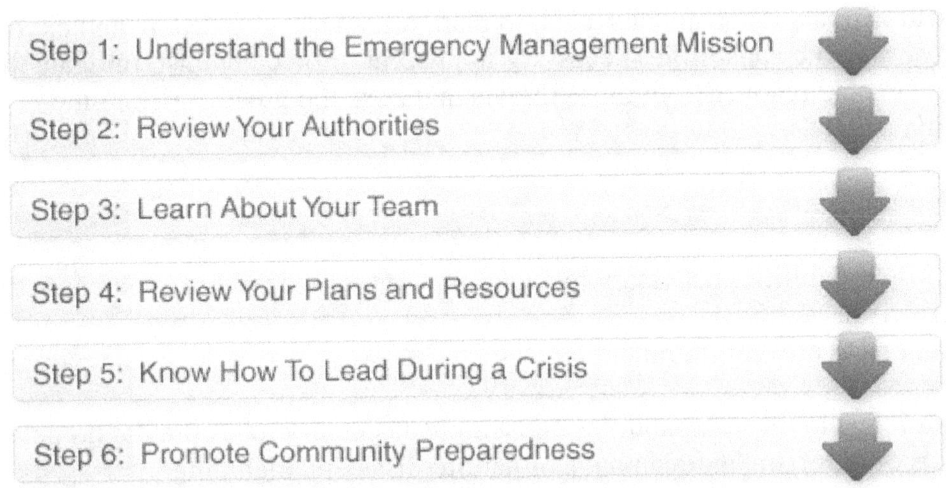

Step 1: Understand the Emergency Management Mission

What is the mission of emergency management within your jurisdiction?

Emergency management coordinates and integrates activities and capabilities needed to mitigate against, prepare for, respond to, and recover from emergencies due to all hazards.

This definition of emergency management is derived from the Definition, Vision, Mission, Principles document developed by the International Association of Emergency Managers in conjunction with FEMA's Emergency Management Higher Education Project.

Key Emergency Management Functions

Emergency management is not just responding to crisis. An effective emergency management program includes the following functions:

- Preparedness
- Prevention
- Protection
- Mitigation
- Response
- Recovery

Preparedness refers to the actions taken to plan, organize, equip, train, and exercise to build and sustain the capabilities necessary to prevent, protect against, mitigate the effects of, respond to, and recover from those threats that pose the greatest risk to the community.

Prevention refers to:

- Those capabilities necessary to avoid, prevent, or stop a threatened or actual act of terrorism.
- Actions to prevent imminent threats.

Protection refers to those capabilities and actions necessary to secure the homeland against acts of terrorism and manmade or natural disasters, including:

- Defense against weapons of mass destruction threats.
- Defense of agriculture and food.
- Protection of leadership and events.
- Critical infrastructure protection.
- Border, maritime, transportation, immigration, and cyber security.

Mitigation refers to those capabilities and actions necessary to reduce loss of life and property by lessening the impact of disasters. Mitigation capabilities include, but are not limited to:

- Community-wide risk reduction projects.
- Efforts to improve the resilience of critical infrastructure and key resource lifelines.

- Risk reduction for specific vulnerabilities from natural hazards or acts of terrorism.
- Initiatives to reduce future risks after a disaster has occurred.

Response refers to those capabilities and actions necessary to save lives, protect property and the environment, and meet basic human needs after an incident has occurred. Response includes:

- Medical care/treatment.
- Mass care.
- Critical infrastructure restoration.
- Incident command and management.

Recovery refers to those capabilities and actions necessary to assist communities affected by an incident to recover effectively. Recovery capabilities include, but are not limited to:

- Rebuilding infrastructure systems.
- Providing adequate interim and long-term housing for survivors.
- Restoring health, social, and community services.
- Promoting economic development.
- Restoring natural and cultural resources.

Integrated Emergency Management

When possible, you should integrate emergency management into daily decisions, not just during times of disaster. While protecting the population is a primary responsibility of government, it cannot be accomplished without building partnerships among disciplines and across all sectors, including the private sector and the media.

Integrated emergency management enables all agencies and entities to work together better by improving coordination and flexibility among varied jurisdictions. Integrated emergency management:

- Addresses all hazards that threaten a community.
- Is useful in all phases of emergency management.
- Knits together all partnerships and participants for a mutual goal.

Step 2: Review Your Authorities

There are many statutes, rules, and regulations related to emergency management. If you have not already done so, make sure to review your authorities for:

- Developing and promulgating emergency plans and standards for emergency management.
- Proclaiming a state of emergency.
- Requesting assistance from other jurisdictions and the State.
- Disseminating information and warnings.
- Designating highways as emergency management routes.
- Imposing restrictions during an emergency (e.g., controlling traffic, closing or restricting areas, or imposing curfew).
- Ordering evacuation and restricting reentry.

Legal Issues Affecting Emergency Management

The following are examples of legal issues that may be addressed in local emergency management ordinances.

- Who has authority to:
    - Develop and promulgate emergency plans and standards for emergency management
    - Proclaim a state of emergency
    - Request assistance from the State
    - Disseminate information and warnings
    - Designate highways as emergency management routes
    - Impose restrictions during an emergency (e.g., control traffic, close or restrict areas, or impose curfew)
    - Order evacuation and restrict reentry
- Requirement to develop local emergency plans
- Declaration of local emergency and activation of emergency operations plan
- Extent of emergency powers
- Use of the Incident Command System during emergencies
- Termination of emergency, time limits
- Evacuations
- Right of entry for inspections
- Contracting for equipment or services during an emergency, authority to waive contracting requirements
- Priority of emergency management contracts over other contracts during an emergency
- Immunity from liability for State or local jurisdiction
- Exemptions from liability for workers, volunteers, and public shelters during an emergency
- Compensation for injuries to emergency management employees and volunteers
- Registration of volunteers

- Labor disputes involving emergency management personnel
- Mutual aid and assistance agreements
- Emergency use of vehicles
- Use of the State traffic patrol during civil disorder
- Emergency temporary locations for State or local government
- Line of succession
- Preservation of essential public records
- Hazardous substances (including radioactive waste emergencies)—notification, emergency response, liability, recovery of expenses
- Reimbursement of costs, loss, or damage during multijurisdictional response
- Adoption of the emergency management plan

Emergency Management Requirements

In addition, local, tribal, and State authorities may require that:

- Officials are trained in emergency management.
- A local emergency operations plan is developed and maintained.
- A director of emergency management is appointed.
- The National Incident Management System (NIMS) is adopted.

Step 3: Learning About Your Team

Taking time to learn about your emergency management team is important. Make sure you understand:

- How the emergency management organization is structured.
- Emergency management roles and responsibilities.
- Reporting authorities.

In an ideal situation, the emergency manager answers directly to the jurisdiction's chief elected official. In this arrangement, the elected official (who is ultimately legally responsible for emergency management in the jurisdiction) has direct access to unfiltered information from the emergency manager.

Emergency Management:

Know Your Team Audio Transcript

MAYOR HOLDEN:
Our team consists of the Mayor's Office of Homeland Security and Emergency Planning. We have also our police department, we have the police chief there, the fire chief, and also emergency medical services, so all of these agencies are our first responders, but we are the only city in the Nation where all four first responder agencies are ranked number one.

NARRATOR:
The mayor evaluated each first responder organization to ensure that he understood their roles when dealing with disasters.

MAYOR HOLDEN:
Whenever it comes down to the police department, people want to be confident that if the lights go out in an area, that they're still safe.

NARRATOR:
Mayor Holden knew that it was essential that each team member shared his ideals.

JEFF LEDUFF:
If you are a new mayor, the first thing you have to do is pick people with your spirit, with your commitment – that understand your mission.

WALTER MONSOUR:
The leader of the governing authority has to act as the CEO, and he has to rely on his officers, of his corporate entity to function in the environment that he had hired them in. You can't micromanage and this mayor didn't micromanage.

NARRATOR:
The relationship the mayor developed among his team is based on an understanding of what each expects of the other.

ED SMITH:
From my experience, I think once a mayor understands the expectations of his emergency response people his ability to handle an emergency becomes better.

NARRATOR:
One critical expectation is for clear and open communications.

JEFF LEDUFF:
Our expectation is this: a level of communication, constant and open communication. Let me know what your expectations are. Let me know what you think about the job we're

doing. It's good and bad. I expect positives and negatives and the mayor has to communicate with me.

ED SMITH:
Because once you handle the communications side of it, then everybody works better together and there is no missing links.

MAYOR HOLDEN:
The police chief expects us to tell them exactly what we need done, and then they look out for a way to accomplish what I've ordered them or asked them to do.

JEFF LEDUFF:
The mayor sets the pace for our communities. As a police chief, I carry it out as it relates to law enforcement and we give him that on a daily basis. In a time of an emergency, he wants us to be that front line.

MAYOR HOLDEN:
So then we have a seamless program here whereby because we're both on the same page on a regular basis, then there's no dispute.

JEFF LEDUFF:
He sets the mission and we run it.

NARRATOR:
To be a better manager, the mayor spent time with team members, learning what they do and how they do it.

ED SMITH:
First of all, the mayor has to understand what each person brings to the table.

WALTER MONSOUR:
A good leader has to learn from those who know more than he or she does, has to trust that individual.

ED SMITH:
He met with us, spent a day of his time going through some scenarios that would bring us to the point of understanding where everybody fit in.

CHAD GUILLOT:
Going out and actually seeing the job that they do I think is very important. They get a real idea of how the operation works, the challenges that we face and even the resources that we have.

WALTER MONSOUR:
So, we knew enough to be dangerous I guess, but more importantly we knew enough to be able to say yes and no.

Step 4: Review Your Plans and Resources

All States have statutory requirements to prepare an emergency operations plan (EOP).
Make sure that your jurisdiction's EOP:

- Addresses all hazards.
- Outlines how all actions will be coordinated.
- Includes plans for protecting the whole community.
- Details who is responsible for carrying out specific actions.
- Identifies the personnel, equipment, facilities, supplies, and other resources
  available.

Other Plans

While many jurisdictions consider the emergency operations plan (EOP) the centerpiece
of their planning effort, it is not the only plan that addresses emergency management
functions. Other types of plans that support and supplement the EOP include:

- Preparedness Plans
- Continuity Plans
- Recovery Plans
- Mitigation Plans
- Prevention and Protection Plans

Preparedness plans address the process for developing and maintaining capabilities for
the whole community both preincident and postincident. Preparedness plans should
address capabilities needed for prevention, protection, response, recovery, and mitigation
activities. These plans include the schedule for identifying and meeting training needs
based on the expectations created by the EOP; the process and schedule for developing,
conducting, and evaluating exercises and correcting identified deficiencies; and plans for
procuring, retrofitting, or building facilities and equipment that could withstand the
effects of the hazards facing the jurisdiction.

Continuity plans outline essential functions that must be performed during an incident
that disrupts normal operations and the methods by which these functions will be
performed. They also describe the process for timely resumption of normal operations

once the emergency has ended. Continuity of operations (COOP) plans address the continued performance of core capabilities and critical operations during any potential incident. Continuity of government (COG) plans address the preservation and/or reconstitution of government to ensure that constitutional, legislative, and/or administrative responsibilities are maintained.

Recovery plans developed prior to a disaster enable jurisdictions to effectively direct recovery activities and expedite a unified recovery effort. Preincident planning performed in conjunction with community development planning helps to establish recovery priorities, incorporate mitigation strategies in the wake of an incident, and identify options and changes that should be considered or implemented after an incident. Postincident community recovery planning serves to integrate the range of complex decisions in the context of the incident and works as the foundation for allocating resources.

Mitigation plans outline a jurisdiction's strategy for mitigating the hazards it faces. The Disaster Mitigation Act of 2000 requires jurisdictions seeking certain disaster assistance funding to have approved mitigation plans. Mitigation planning is often a long-term effort and may be part of or tied to the jurisdiction's strategic development plan or similar documents. Mitigation planning committees may differ from operational planning teams in that they include zoning boards, floodplain managers, and individuals with long-term cultural or economic interests. Existing plans for mitigating hazards are relevant to an EOP since both originate from a hazard-based analysis and share similar component requirements.

Prevention and protection plans typically tend to be more facility focused and procedural or tactical in their content. Common jurisdictional prevention and protection plans include fusion center operations plans, sector-specific or CIKR security plans, and incident-specific contingency action plans.

Incident Command System (ICS)

When meeting with your emergency response team, you may hear the acronym "ICS." The Incident Command System (ICS) is a standardized, on-scene, all-hazards incident management approach that:

- Allows for the integration of facilities, equipment, personnel, procedures, and communications operating within a common organizational structure.
- Enables a coordinated response among various jurisdictions and functional agencies, both public and private.
- Establishes common processes for planning and managing resources.

ICS is flexible and can be used for incidents of any type, scope, and complexity.

ICS Management Characteristics

ICS is based on the following 14 proven management characteristics that contribute to the strength and efficiency of the overall system:

- Common Terminology
- Modular Organization
- Management by Objectives
- Incident Action Planning
- Manageable Span of Control
- Incident Facilities and Locations
- Comprehensive Resource Management
- Integrated Communications
- Establishment and Transfer of Command
- Chain of Command and Unity of Command
- Unified Command
- Accountability
- Dispatch/Deployment
- Information and Intelligence Management

Common Terminology: ICS establishes common terminology that allows diverse incident management and support organizations to work together across a wide variety of incident management functions and hazard scenarios. This common terminology covers the following:

- **Organizational Functions:** Major functions and functional units with incident management responsibilities are named and defined. Terminology for the organizational elements is standard and consistent.
- **Resource Descriptions:** Major resources—including personnel, facilities, and major equipment and supply items—that support incident management activities are given common names and are "typed" with respect to their capabilities, to help avoid confusion and to enhance interoperability.
- **Incident Facilities:** Common terminology is used to designate the facilities in the vicinity of the incident area that will be used during the course of the incident.

Incident response communications (during exercises and actual incidents) should feature plain language commands so they will be able to function in a multijurisdiction environment. Field manuals and training should be revised to reflect the plain language standard.

Modular Organization: The ICS organizational structure develops in a modular fashion based on the size and complexity of the incident, as well as the specifics of the hazard environment created by the incident. When needed, separate functional elements can be established, each of which may be further subdivided to enhance internal organizational management and external coordination. Responsibility for the establishment and expansion of the ICS modular organization ultimately rests with Incident Command, which bases the ICS organization on the requirements of the situation. As incident complexity increases, the organization expands from the top down as functional responsibilities are delegated. Concurrently with structural expansion, the number of management and supervisory positions expands to address the requirements of the incident adequately.

Management by Objectives: Management by objectives is communicated throughout the entire ICS organization and includes:

- Establishing overarching incident objectives.
- Developing strategies based on overarching incident objectives.
- Developing and issuing assignments, plans, procedures, and protocols.
- Establishing specific, measurable tactics or tasks for various incident management functional activities, and directing efforts to accomplish them, in support of defined strategies.
- Documenting results to measure performance and facilitate corrective actions.

Incident Action Planning: Centralized, coordinated incident action planning should guide all response activities. An Incident Action Plan (IAP) provides a concise, coherent means of capturing and communicating the overall incident priorities, objectives, and strategies in the contexts of both operational and support activities. Every incident must have an action plan. However, not all incidents require written plans. The need for written plans and attachments is based on the requirements of the incident and the decision of the Incident Commander or Unified Command. Most initial response operations are not captured with a formal IAP. However, if an incident is likely to extend beyond one operational period, become more complex, or involve multiple jurisdictions and/or agencies, preparing a written IAP will become increasingly important to maintain effective, efficient, and safe operations.

Manageable Span of Control: Span of control is key to effective and efficient incident management. Supervisors must be able to adequately supervise and control their subordinates, as well as communicate with and manage all resources under their supervision. In ICS, the span of control of any individual with incident management supervisory responsibility should range from 3 to 7 subordinates, with 5 being optimal. During a large-scale law enforcement operation, 8 to 10 subordinates may be optimal. The type of incident, nature of the task, hazards and safety factors, and distances between personnel and resources all influence span-of-control considerations.

Incident Facilities and Locations: Various types of operational support facilities are established in the vicinity of an incident, depending on its size and complexity, to accomplish a variety of purposes. The Incident Command will direct the identification and location of facilities based on the requirements of the situation. Typical designated facilities include Incident Command Posts, Bases, Camps, Staging Areas, mass casualty triage areas, point-of-distribution sites, and others as required.

Comprehensive Resource Management: Maintaining an accurate and up-to-date picture of resource utilization is a critical component of incident management and emergency response. Resources to be identified in this way include personnel, teams, equipment, supplies, and facilities available or potentially available for assignment or allocation. Resource management is described in detail in Component III.

Integrated Communications: Incident communications are facilitated through the development and use of a common communications plan and interoperable communications processes and architectures. The ICS 205 form is available to assist in developing a common communications plan. This integrated approach links the operational and support units of the various agencies involved and is necessary to maintain communications connectivity and discipline and to enable common situational awareness and interaction. Preparedness planning should address the equipment, systems, and protocols necessary to achieve integrated voice and data communications.

Establishment and Transfer of Command: The command function must be clearly established from the beginning of incident operations. The agency with primary jurisdictional authority over the incident designates the individual at the scene responsible for establishing command. When command is transferred, the process must include a briefing that captures all essential information for continuing safe and effective operations.

Chain of Command and Unity of Command:

- **Chain of Command:** Chain of command refers to the orderly line of authority within the ranks of the incident management organization.
- **Unity of Command:** Unity of command means that all individuals have a designated supervisor to whom they report at the scene of the incident. These principles clarify reporting relationships and eliminate the confusion caused by multiple, conflicting directives. Incident managers at all levels must be able to direct the actions of all personnel under their supervision.

Unified Command: In incidents involving multiple jurisdictions, a single jurisdiction with multiagency involvement, or multiple jurisdictions with multiagency involvement, Unified Command allows agencies with different legal, geographic, and functional authorities and responsibilities to work together effectively without affecting individual agency authority, responsibility, or accountability.

Accountability: Effective accountability of resources at all jurisdictional levels and within individual functional areas during incident operations is essential. Adherence to the following ICS principles and processes helps to ensure accountability:

- Resource Check-In/Check-Out Procedures
- Incident Action Planning
- Unity of Command
- Personal Responsibility

- Span of Control
- Resource Tracking

Dispatch/Deployment: Resources should respond only when requested or when dispatched by an appropriate authority through established resource management systems. Resources not requested must refrain from spontaneous deployment to avoid overburdening the recipient and compounding accountability challenges.

Information and Intelligence Management: The incident management organization must establish a process for gathering, analyzing, assessing, sharing, and managing incident-related information and intelligence.

Visit Emergency Management Facilities

Before a crisis, you should be familiar with the physical layout and roles of the emergency resources and facilities in your jurisdiction. These facilities may include the following:

- **Communications/Dispatch Center:** The agency or interagency dispatch center, 911 call center, or emergency control or command dispatch center that handles emergency calls from the public and communication with emergency management personnel.
- **Emergency Operations Center (EOC):** The physical location at which the coordination of information and resources to **support** incident management (on-scene operations) activities normally takes place.

  An EOC may be a temporary facility or may be located in a more central or permanently established facility, perhaps at a higher level of organization within a jurisdiction.

Emergency Management: Emergency Operations Center Audio Transcript

JOANNE H. MOREAU:
Our motto is "Prepare for the worst" because the worst can happen – we've seen that.

NARRATOR:
The emergency management agency for Baton Rouge is called the Mayor's Office of Homeland Security and Emergency Preparedness.

MAYOR HOLDEN:
You're expecting them to lay out the blueprint for everybody. When you sit around this table, they know and have put in place every agency that's needed to keep the media updated and people updated on what situation is occurring. They know where doctors need to be placed, they need to know what briefings we need, if medical supplies need to come in, they know how to set up a system to alert us as to where evacuees are located, and so they become that center that virtually guides every aspect of emergency preparedness.

JOANNE H. MOREAU:
During an activation, the entire upper floor becomes activated with just about every type of agency whether it's local, State, or Federal known to man.

WALTER MONSOUR:
I think it's very critical that once you're in a crisis situation that you try to put everybody in the same room.

DAVID GUILLORY:
The major goal with an EOC is to get everybody on the same playing field, let everybody communicate.

MAYOR HOLDEN:
You have all of these different emergency response agencies and in our situation they're all housed around a table, probably about 50 different agencies.

CHAD GUILLOT:
This facility provides basically the connectivity that we need, the face to face that we need to make a big difference in mitigating an emergency or a big disaster.

ED SMITH:
And each discipline has a chair that they're responsible for – the police, fire, DPW, hospitals, industrial, sheriffs – and so that's how we manage this room.

JEFF LEDUFF:
We stay here from the start of the event to the end of the event and that communication and that availability of people, to put hands on and get problems resolved, is imperative.

OBIE CAMBRE:
You're comfortable talking to each other and asking those things that, they're really "make sense" things, but you don't get locked up in bureaucracy.

CHAD GUILLOT:
If you want to know if something is going on, this is the best place to be because all of the information from all the different agencies from both public and private are coming into this facility.

JOANNE H. MOREAU:
We focus a lot on making sure that we have a very accurate and timely information process of information dissemination.

JEFF LEDUFF:
We are the first line of information for the rest of the team because we're out there all the time.

JOANNE H. MOREAU:
We are able to work with all agencies and give a real solid, unified message.

MAYOR HOLDEN:
Sometimes you have to get your story out very quickly.

JOANNE H. MOREAU:
The media is embedded in our emergency operations center, they have access to the officials.

MAYOR HOLDEN:
By having that access, it really helped us to quell the various rumors that were out there and we were able to keep the situation calm.

Resource Management Systems

After becoming familiar with your jurisdiction plans and facilities, it is important to review the resource management systems to ensure that they include procedures for:

- Describing, inventorying, requesting, and tracking resources.
- Activating and dispatching resources.
- Managing volunteers and donations.
- Demobilizing or recalling resources.
- Financial tracking, reimbursement, and reporting.

In addition, check that the jurisdiction has adequate mutual aid agreements for obtaining resources, facilities, services, and other required support from other jurisdictions or organizations.

Mutual Aid Agreements

What Is a Mutual Aid Agreement?

A mutual aid agreement is a legal document that provides a formal framework for assistance between parties. A mutual aid agreement typically outlines request and response procedures and liability, reimbursement, and worker's compensation procedures.

Agreements should be documented in writing in order to reduce or eliminate the possibility of misunderstandings between the participating parties.

It is critical to identify the legal authorities that authorize a jurisdiction's participation in a mutual aid agreement. These types of legal authorities may be in the form of:

- Authorizing resolutions.
- Statutes.
- Ordinances.

Mutual Aid Agreement Contents

Regardless of what format is used, a mutual aid agreement should include the following components:

- **Purpose and Scope:** Sometimes called a Preamble, the Purpose and Scope section sets the tone for the agreement. This section should include:
  - The need for an agreement,
  - The range of incidents in which it is applicable, and
  - The member organizations.
- **References and Authorities:** References and authorities refer to existing statutes or regulations that authorize mutual aid contracts or compacts. This section also includes a listing of any prior agreements that are mentioned in the mutual aid agreement, such as those that will be superseded or will in some way affect the new agreement. By including a References and Authorities section, applicable statutes can be quickly accessed by interested parties.
- **Definitions:** Defining key terms helps avoid differences in interpretation. For example, words like "emergency" can have different meanings for different organizations. Defining terms is especially important for complex agreements that go into small levels of detail. If levels of aid are to be determined by the agreement itself, then clear definitions must be in place.
- **Effect on Existing Agreements:** Comprehensive legal review should determine if any serious conflicts exist with existing agreements. A clause should be included that states what effect the new agreement has on existing agreements. New agreements should replace older agreements in order to avoid conflict and potential disputes between parties. In general, new agreements should not prohibit future supplemental agreements between all or some of the parties to the agreement.
- **Roles and Responsibilities:** The Roles and Responsibilities section should include the roles and responsibilities of each party. This section usually contains information about who can activate the agreement.

- **Mediation/Dispute Resolution:** The Mediation/Dispute Resolution section should include information on how disputes will be resolved. This may include the use of mediation, arbitration, and/or court of jurisdiction.
- **Training and Exercises:** Mutual aid agreements should include language on training and exercises, including how often training and exercises will be conducted. The agreement should mandate joint planning, training, and exercises with the same liability immunity as if it were a real emergency.
- **Liability and Insurance:** The Liability and Insurance section of a mutual aid agreement should spell out the liability of all parties and provide guidance for arbitration or resolution of any claims. Legal counsel should play a lead role in drafting and reviewing all agreement language related to these issues.

  In most cases, agreements should indemnify mutual aid partners from any liability from alleged negligence, except for cases of gross negligence and/or willful misconduct, occurring during a mutual aid response.

  Insurance, including worker's compensation insurance, should be required of all parties, and insurers must be made aware of mutual aid requirements.

  Some tribal governments may request or even require resolution of legal disputes within a Tribal Court System, particularly if the event leading to the dispute occurs within the tribe's jurisdiction.
- **Limitations:** The Limitations section of a mutual aid agreement specifies the conditions under which a participating jurisdiction's obligation to provide assistance and resources may or may not be limited.
- **License, Certificate, and Permit Portability**: The License, Certificate, and Permit Portability section specifies the conditions under which a person or entity who holds a license, certificate, or other permit is deemed to be licensed, certified, or permitted in the jurisdiction requesting assistance.

  In general, it is best to allow for a responder's license, certificate, or permit to be valid in the requesting jurisdiction. For example, a law enforcement official from County X should have the same arrest powers in County Y that he or she has in County X.
- **Terms and Conditions:** The purpose of this section is to specify the duration or the life expectancy of the agreement. It is important to clarify expectations of all signatories about the lifespan of the agreement and how it will be renewed.

  It is recommended that the agreement have a beginning and an end date. In addition, if necessary to renew the agreement, there should be stipulations as to what actions need to take place to renew or there should be language indicating that the renewal is automatic.
- **Reimbursement:** The goal of this section is to clarify issues over reimbursement such as:
    - Who is responsible for paying for specific resources.
    - What expenses are eligible for reimbursement.

- o   What triggers the reimbursement provision of the agreement. (For example, some agreements are written in such a way that for the first 24 hours of aid provided, there is no cost to the requesting jurisdiction. It is only after that initial period that reimbursement becomes an issue.)
- **Severability:** The Severability section of a mutual aid agreement addresses how one or more of the signatories can leave the agreement while leaving the rest of the agreement intact. This section can also make provisions for cases in which an article of the agreement is found invalid. In this case, the Severability section will include language that ensures the rest of the agreement remains binding for the rest of the parties.

Training and Exercises

Plans are only as effective as the people who implement them. Make sure that all personnel with roles in emergency management and incident response—including persons in leadership positions, such as elected and appointed officials—receive periodic training.

In addition, your jurisdiction should have an exercise plan. Exercises help to:

- Test and evaluate plans, policies, and procedures.
- Identify resource gaps and shortfalls.
- Improve interagency coordination and communication.
- Clarify roles and responsibilities.
- Gain public recognition that the government has taken steps to protect the safety of community members and responders—an opportunity to showcase what you can do.

Training Options

Type	Appropriate for Providing . . .
Classroom	A knowledge base on new or revised processes and/or procedures. The skills needed to perform tasks that would be done manually (e.g., analyzing information from documents provided) or with equipment contained in the classroom (e.g., computers, telephones) or on the job.
Independent Study	Knowledge acquisition at a pace that is comfortable for the student. An opportunity to learn and apply knowledge and skills (e.g., through a tutorial) in a self-paced environment.

On-the-Job Training	An opportunity to learn and perform tasks in a real-life environment with the supervision of an expert performer. (A related form of training is the practicum, which is designed to give the learner supervised practical application of a previously or concurrently studied theory. Another option, shadowing, allows the learner to observe an expert performer on the job.)
Briefings	New information, usually at a high level, presented to all persons who have a need to know or use the information. Briefings are often provided to large groups and include a question-and-answer session.
Workshops	Opportunities for small numbers of job performers to discuss issues and apply knowledge and skills to solving problems or producing a product. Workshops are generally highly structured and their outputs are usually a product that meets specified criteria (e.g., a list of assumptions that will be used as a basis for developing the emergency operations plan).
Job Aids	Quick references that are intended to be used on the job. Common job aids include checklists, worksheets, standard operating procedures, reference guides, etc.

Discussion-Based Exercises

Discussion-based exercises familiarize participants with current plans, policies, agreements, and procedures, or may be used to develop new plans, policies, agreements, and procedures.

Type	**Description**
Seminar	A seminar is an informal discussion, designed to orient participants to new or updated plans, policies, or procedures (e.g., a seminar to review a new evacuation standard operating procedure).
Workshop	A workshop resembles a seminar, but is employed to build specific products, such as a draft plan or policy.
Tabletop Exercise	A tabletop exercise involves key personnel discussing simulated scenarios in an informal setting. Tabletop exercises can be used to assess plans, policies, and procedures.
Game	A game is a simulation of operations that often involves two or more teams, usually in a competitive environment, using rules, data, and procedures designed to depict an actual or assumed real-life situation.

Operations-Based Exercises

Operations-based exercises validate plans, policies, agreements, and procedures; clarify roles and responsibilities; and identify resource gaps in an operational environment.

Type	Description
Drill	A drill is a coordinated, supervised activity usually employed to test a single, specific operation or function within a single entity (e.g., a fire department conducts a decontamination drill).
Functional Exercise	A functional exercise examines and/or validates the coordination, command, and control between various multiagency coordination centers (e.g., EOC or Joint Field Office). A functional exercise does not involve any "boots on the ground" (i.e., first responders or emergency officials responding to an incident in real time).
Full-Scale Exercise	A full-scale exercise is a multiagency, multijurisdiction, multidiscipline exercise involving functional and "boots on the ground" response (e.g., firefighters decontaminating mock disaster survivors).

Homeland Security Exercise and Evaluation Program (HSEEP)

The Homeland Security Exercise and Evaluation Program (HSEEP) is a capabilities- and performance-based exercise program that provides a standardized policy, methodology, and language for designing, developing, conducting, and evaluating all exercises.

HSEEP also facilitates the creation of self-sustaining, capabilities-based exercise programs by providing tools and resources such as policy and guidance, training, technology, and direct exercise support. This blended approach to HSEEP implementation promotes exercise expertise, while advancing a standardized means of assessing and improving preparedness across the Nation. HSEEP provides common processes, consistent terminology, tools, and policies that are practical and flexible for all exercise planners.

The HSEEP volumes deliver exercise program guidelines that capture lessons learned and best practices of existing exercise approaches, while suggesting strategies that align exercise programs within a broader spectrum of preparedness activities, such as training, planning, and equipment purchases. The HSEEP approach can be adapted to a variety of scenarios and events.

Emergency Management:

Setting High Standards Audio Transcript

NARRATOR:
The mayor knows he has to support his team by providing the training, equipment, and technology necessary to deal with a crisis situation.

JEFF LEDUFF:
When I took this job and the mayor came into his function, we were 20 years behind everybody else's technology. We have new buildings now, our technology is state of the art. We have wi-fied vehicles, laptops that we can air card, and each vehicle is its own hotspot in this community so communications between interagency is simultaneous. He's getting us the funds to pay our people properly and make sure we have good benefits and the buildings we need to work in to be that professional police department and carry out the tasks in a professional manner. So that support is important.

NARRATOR:
Mayor Holden has established high standards for his team and the team works to live up to those standards.

ED SMITH:
The mayor has a high expectation and we treasure that because it makes us perform better, train better, and do the things that we need and we don't have a problem with having high expectations.

JOANNE H. MOREAU:
Our leadership, our elected officials are engaged not only in supporting us financially but also engaged in our processes.

JEFF LEDUFF:
Our team is a good team because we have a good leader . . . and I am just a chip off my mayor's block.

Step 5: Know How To Lead During a Crisis

During a crisis, providing leadership is the most important role of senior officials. Senior officials provide leadership by:

- Delegating authority to on-scene responders.
- Instilling confidence in the public that the incident is being managed effectively.
- Making policy decisions and securing needed resources.
- Building partnerships and alliances.

Your role is not to set incident objectives or direct tactical operations. Rather, officials delegate this role to Incident Commanders and first responders who are qualified to manage the incident.

Emergency Management: Leadership Audio Transcript

NARRATOR:
During an incident, you will find the mayor providing policy guidance and leadership at the Emergency Operations Center.

MAYOR HOLDEN:
I've been here for a number of hurricanes, and a number of events, but I don't go home. If I have to take a nap, I take a nap here, but I'm here virtually around the clock, so they know that if there's a decision to be made, then I'm right here.

JOANNE H. MOREAU:
Having an elected official that is familiar with the process, that understands the needs of the community as well as understands what resources are available within the response community and marrying those two together, it's like a secret to success.

WALTER MONSOUR:
People to this day, five years after Katrina, three years after Gustav, still stop the mayor and I on the street and say thank you.

MAYOR HOLDEN:
It's interesting in Baton Rouge how people now say "Once we hear from you, then we feel confident about what's going on," so what happens is they now have entrusted that person to become a leader.

NARRATOR:
Mayor Holden expanded his team to include the local government agencies that the first responders rely upon.

DAVID GUILLORY:
In emergency situations it's good to have a close relationship with your city departments so everything can get back to normal as quick as possible.

MAYOR HOLDEN:
Fire department also, especially if you have electrical lines falling down, they have to work with our Department of Public Works.

DAVID GUILLORY:
The Department of Public Works will maintain the infrastructure so people can move on with their life as they know it and in emergencies usually you will lose services and the quicker you can get services back up and running the better for everyone.

NARRATOR:
The mayor and his staff formed partnerships with nongovernmental organizations and the private sector.

JOANNE H. MOREAU:
You need to look at your private stakeholders, your nonprofit entities, your military personnel, your other partners that—nontraditional kind of partners, you know—innovative ways to be able to compliment limited resources with some outside of what you normally would consider.

MAYOR HOLDEN:
The business community is looking for ways to make sure they can keep themselves going as well. You know if there are no utilities, then they have a problem. They're also concerned about their employees getting to work. So if the employees don't show up, there's a problem. Then you have to make sure that we do not do anything that will adversely impact them, so it boils down to a team working together to make sure that we're still vibrant, because you still have an economy to deal with. And so if the businesses are down, then the bottom line at the end of the month for any city or any parish or any county is going to be your tax revenues are down.

JEFF JENKINS:
Information from local elected officials on a regular basis is really critical.

ADAM KNAPP:
The leadership of the elected official in getting people back to normal living conditions or as close as possible, as quickly as possible, is important for the operations of the company because the labor that they need to have back in place to restart their companies too so there's a lot of interconnection of the networks there.

JOANNE H. MOREAU:
It's really, really important to have the community engaged in the process because government can't do everything for everyone.

MIKE MANNING:
It's most important that we have our people prepared and we don't forget the underserved people who can't prepare. The mayor is very engaged with the nonprofits. He does everything he can to help us because he knows how important we are to the community. The nonprofits can be tremendous resources to help in a response, to help with rebuilding, to help with long-term recovery. We are assisting people on a daily basis, that's what we do and that really is our skill set and that's what we can bring to the table to help mayors, to help emergency managers, to really make a difference in response.

Decision-making

One important function for senior officials is to make policy decisions. You may want to use the following criteria when making decisions and establishing priorities:

Life Safety

- Threat to responders
- Threat to public

Incident Stabilization

- Damage potential
- Incident complexity
- Infrastructure protection

Property Conservation

- Real property threatened
- Environmental impact
- Economic impact

Common Incident Response Actions

Specific response actions will vary depending upon the scope and nature of the incident. Response actions are based on the objectives established by the Incident Command. Response actions include, but are not limited to:

- Warning the public and providing accessible emergency public information.
- Implementing evacuation and sheltering plans that include provisions for special needs populations and household pets.
- Sheltering evacuees.
- Performing search and rescue.
- Treating the injured.
- Providing law enforcement and investigation.

- Controlling hazards (extinguishing fires, containing hazardous materials spills, etc.).
- Ensuring responder safety and health.

Requesting Additional Resources

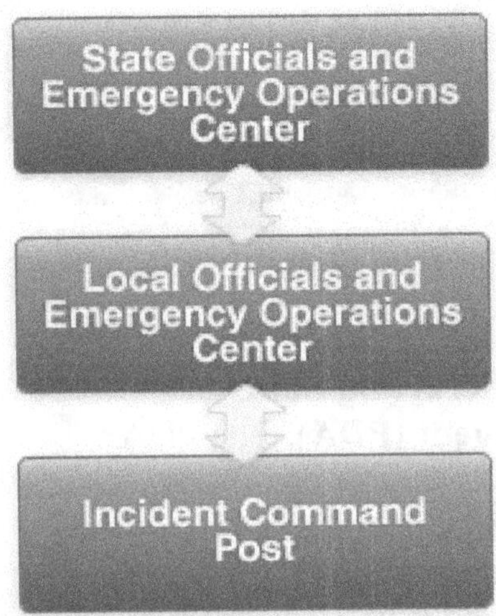

In the vast majority of incidents, local resources and local mutual aid agreements provide the first line of emergency management and incident response.

In other instances, incidents that begin with a single response within a single jurisdiction rapidly expand requiring significant additional resources and operational support.

Jurisdictions may request additional assistance from the State. If State officials cannot fulfill resource requests, they may use interstate mutual aid agreements, the private sector, and nongovernmental organizations to help fulfill needs.

Requesting Federal Assistance

The Federal Government may provide assistance in the form of funding, resources, and critical services. The intention of the Federal Government in these situations is not to command the response, but rather to support the affected local, tribal, and/or State governments.

When it is clear that State capabilities will be exceeded, the Governor can request Federal assistance, including assistance under the **Robert T. Stafford Disaster Relief and Emergency Assistance Act** (the Stafford Act).

Stafford Act Declaration Process

There is a four-step process for an incident to be declared a Presidential major disaster.

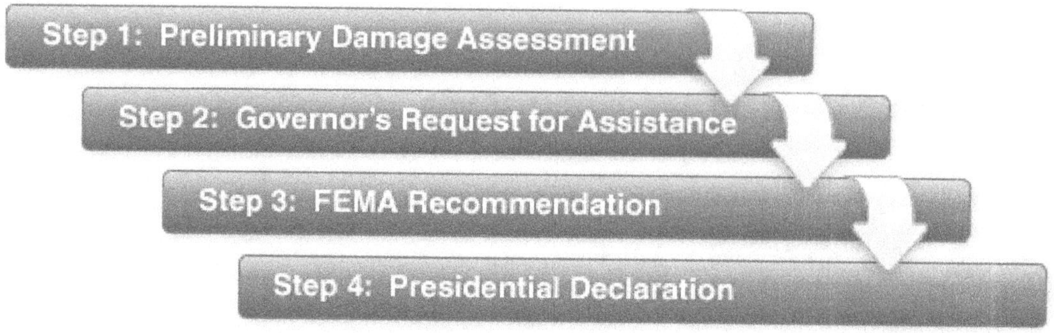

Step 1: Preliminary Damage Assessment

After the Governor requests Federal assistance, **FEMA/Federal and State representatives complete a Preliminary Damage Assessment (PDA).** The PDA:

- Documents the impact of the event and estimates initial damage.
- Establishes a foundation for the Governor to request assistance.
- Provides background for FEMA's analysis of the request.

Step 2: Governor's Request for Assistance

Next, **the Governor requests assistance.** The Governor's request, by law, must:

- State that the Governor has taken appropriate action and directed execution of the State emergency operations plan.
- Certify that the incident is of such severity and magnitude that State and local resources are inadequate.
- Include a damage estimate.
- Describe the State and local resources committed to response and recovery.
- Describe the assistance being requested and agree to cost-sharing provisions.

Step 3: FEMA Recommendation

Third, **FEMA reviews the request and makes a recommendation.** The Governor's request is addressed to the President through the FEMA Regional Administrator. The FEMA Regional Office also completes its analysis and recommendation. FEMA Headquarters then reviews the Governor's request as well as the analysis and recommendation, to ensure the request meets Stafford Act requirements. The FEMA Administrator then recommends a course of action to the President.

Step 4: Presidential Declaration

Fourth, **the President makes a major disaster declaration, if warranted.** The President decides whether to declare that a major disaster exists. If a declaration is issued, assistance is made available under the Stafford Act. A Federal Coordinating Officer (FCO) is designated to oversee the disaster operations.

Typically, this process may take several days. In cases where an immediate Federal response is needed to save lives or protect public health and safety, an expedited disaster request may start the process within hours. When there is a predicted disaster threat (i.e., hurricane, flooding), the President can declare the disaster preincident.

Public Information: Speaking With One Voice

People during disasters are overwhelmed. As a senior official, you must ensure that information provided to the public is:

- Accurate and timely.
- Consistent.
- Accessible to the whole community.
- Focused on the immediate needs.
- Helpful for building confidence in the response and recovery efforts.

During an incident, your jurisdiction may establish or participate in a Joint Information Center (JIC) to help ensure that everyone is speaking with one voice.

Role of the Public Information Officer (PIO)

The PIO advises the Incident Commander on all public information matters relating to the management of the incident. The PIO handles inquiries from the media, the public, and elected officials; emergency public information and warnings; rumor monitoring and response; media monitoring; and other functions required to gather, verify, coordinate, and disseminate accurate, accessible, and timely information related to the incident, particularly regarding information on public health, safety, and protection.

Joint Information Center (JIC)

The JIC:

- Is a physical location with tools to enhance the flow of public information.
- Provides a central working facility where PIOs can gather.
- Allows PIOs to handle increased information needs by the media and the public during and after a crisis.
- Maximizes communication between different PIOs while minimizing conflicting or inaccurate information being sent to the media and the public.

- Can provide "one-stop shopping" for the media. This makes it more enticing for the media to focus on "official" information rather than scattering for other parts of the story.

While a single JIC location is preferable, the system is flexible and adaptable enough to accommodate virtual or multiple JIC locations, as required.

- If possible, it is advised to have location(s) identified that could be used as a JIC before an incident occurs—ideally, collocated with or in close proximity to the EOC. It is important that these locations meet the working needs of the PIO function and allow easy access for the media.
- After a JIC has been identified, it is recommended to have appropriate equipment and other resources available and operational. The PIO should develop standard operating procedures on the actual use of the JIC and the equipment and staff that may be needed.

Step 6: Promote Community Preparedness

A resilient community is one that can adapt to changing conditions and withstand and rapidly recover from disruption due to emergencies. Preparedness must take place at all levels:

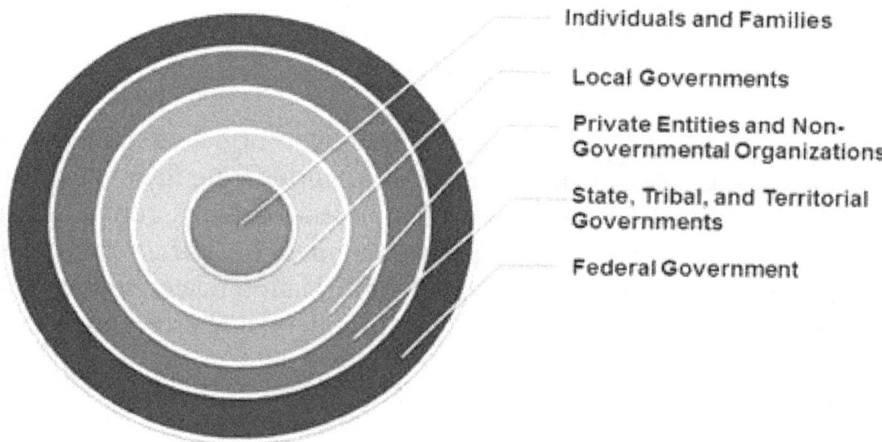

As a senior official, you play an important role in promoting community preparedness.

Individuals and Households

Individuals and households are at the core of our Nation's preparedness. A community's ability to respond to or recover from a disaster depends on the level of preparedness of every member.

However, a 2009 Citizen Corps national survey found that 29 percent of Americans have not prepared because they think that emergency responders will help them, and that over 60 percent expect to rely on emergency responders in the first 72 hours following a disaster.

The reality is that in a complex disaster, first responders and emergency workers may not be able to reach everyone right away. In addition, providers may not be able to restore critical services, such as power, immediately.

Individual and community preparedness is critical. A ready resource for developing an education and outreach program is available in the independent study course IS-909, Community Preparedness: Simple Activities for Everyone. This course provides a wide range of activities for promoting personal and organizational preparedness.

Preparedness Topics

Below is a list of preparedness activities included in the *Community Preparedness: Simple Activities for Everyone* program:

Core Preparedness Topics

Title	Information and Activities on . . .	Approx. Length
Preparedness on a Shoestring	Creating a no-cost or low-cost disaster kit	30–60 minutes
Where Is Everybody?	Developing a communications plan	20 minutes
Who Can You Count On? Who Counts on You?	Establishing a personal support network	20 minutes
Easy Out: Getting to Safety	Planning for and practicing an evacuation	30 minutes
Storm Safe — Sheltering in Place	Staying safe when evacuation is not an option	20–40 minutes
Disaster Plan Dress Rehearsal	Practicing your disaster plan	30–60 minutes

Hazard-Reduction Topics

Title	Information and Activities on . . .	Approx. Length
Hunting Home Hazards	Identifying and reducing home hazards	30–60 minutes
An Ounce of Fire Prevention	Identifying and reducing fire risks	30 minutes
Putting Out Fires	Using a fire extinguisher	30–60 minutes
Home Safe Home	Implementing simple risk-reduction (mitigation) measures	30–60 minutes
Safeguarding Your Valuables	Protecting important items and documents	30 minutes

Specialized Preparedness Topics

Title	Information and Activities on . . .	Approx. Length
Pet/Service Animal Preparedness	Taking care of pets and service animals during a disaster	30 minutes
Rx for Readiness	Starting a "Stay Healthy" Kit and plan	30 minutes
Going Off Grid: Utility Outages	Preparing for utility outages	20–40 minutes
Coming Home After a Disaster	Planning for recovery from disaster	20 minutes
Preparedness: The Whole Community	Understanding emergency management and response roles and getting involved	30–90 minutes

You can mix and match the topics based on the needs of your audience. In addition, you may adjust the times by modifying the activities demonstrated during the session.

Community Preparedness Principles

Citizen Corps, an organization created to help coordinate volunteer activities, established the following community preparedness principles:

- **Collaboration:** Government must collaborate with community leaders from all sectors for effective planning and capacity building.
- **Integration:** Nongovernmental assets and resources must be fully integrated into government plans, preparations, and disaster response.
- **Personal/Organizational Preparedness:** Everyone in America should be fully aware, trained, and practiced on how to prevent, protect, mitigate, prepare for, and respond to all threats and hazards.
- **Volunteer Service:** Citizen activism and volunteer service provide ongoing support for community safety and critical surge capacity in response and recovery.

Volunteer Service Resources

Citizens Corps	Engages individuals in preparedness activities.
Community Emergency Response Team (CERT) Program	Trains people to be better prepared to respond to emergency situations.
Fire Corps	Supports and augments fire and emergency services through volunteers and training.
Medical Reserve Corps	Coordinates volunteer service by practicing and retired health professionals.
Volunteers in Police Service	Helps law enforcement departments develop or enhance volunteer programs.
USAonWatch	Conducts Neighborhood Watch "eyes and ears" training.

Emergency Management: Preparedness Audio Transcript

NARRATOR:
This presentation tells the story of how Mayor Melvin "Kip" Holden succeeded in engaging the City of Baton Rouge, in East Baton Rouge Parish, to be better prepared.

JOANNE H. MOREAU:
It's really, really important to have the community engaged in the process, because government can't do everything for everyone.

NARRATOR:
While responding to disasters, Mayor Holden and his staff began to realize that many of the issues they faced repeatedly could be eliminated if the public was better prepared.

RANNAH GRAY:
Our current mayor, Kip Holden, worked with his staff at the Mayor's Office of Homeland Security and Emergency Preparedness with an idea that we need more public education.

NARRATOR:
The first step was to ask others how outreach and education could be improved.

JOANNE H. MOREAU:
While our message was kind of sporadic and always public safety, we weren't quite sure if we were doing the best that we could. So that was the basis for our survey, to find out: where do we go from here?

RANNAH GRAY:
And one of the things that really came to light was there's such a need, so many people didn't know what to do, didn't have a plan, separated from families, didn't know how to get in contact, separated from prescription medicines.

NARRATOR:
Based on survey results, the Mayor's Office developed an outreach campaign for the whole community known as Red Stick Ready.

RANNAH GRAY:
We like to say that our audience is everyone. And we have lots of messages and we try to target. If we're talking about a senior population, we go work with our Council on Aging on any programs that might target seniors. If we're talking to children, we try to get into the schools.

JOANNE H. MOREAU:
Working with the children, and with such an emphasis on the children, we wanted a tool that could reach them.

MAYOR HOLDEN:
We have what they call Mayor Mouse, and Mayor Mouse basically is operated to go to various schools. In a span of, I think, 2 months, we took in roughly about almost 3,000 kids at various sites to talk to them about different safety things.

JOANNE H. MOREAU:
So Mayor Mouse, our Mayor, along with the real mayor actually goes to that event and

interacts with the people that are present. You'll be quite surprised at how the elected official mouse makes all the difference with the children.

JOANNE H. MOREAU:
The children are selected by the teacher and come in and for several hours, run the city and the fire chief works with the child that is the fire chief. So there's a lot about interaction, they learn about their position prior to an event, they have to do public speaking because there's a series of briefings that are held and the kids have to stand up and talk about what they're doing as the fire chief.

MAYOR HOLDEN:
We'll often talk to young kids and say to them that you need to plan an evacuation route. We talk to parents and say you need to plan an evacuation route. And then we feature the fire chief and we feature hazmat and other components of the fire department to talk about fire safety.

RANNAH GRAY:
It's so important for local officials to communicate directly with their community and with the public. There's no better spokespersons that they want to see and hear from than their local elected officials, and this can be just highly effective in carrying this message out to the community.

RANNAH GRAY:
We feel that we've really made strides in teaching the public.

JOANNE H. MOREAU:
Where we see Red Stick Ready going is that other communities, and we do share with a lot of communities, that we have a common message about preparedness.

RANNAH GRAY:
We won't be satisfied until everyone that we talk to is ready for an emergency.

JOANNE H. MOREAU:
It's community preparedness, and it's a community, one household at a time.

Additional Resources

Below are additional resources that you may want to consult:

- The National Incident Management System (NIMS) provides a template for the management of incidents.
- The National Response Framework (NRF) provides the structure and mechanisms for national-level policy for incident management.
- The National Disaster Recovery Framework is a guide that enables effective recovery support to disaster-impacted jurisdictions.
- Comprehensive Preparedness Guide 101 is designed to assist jurisdictions with developing operations plans.
- The IS-909 - Community Preparedness: Implementing Simple Activities for Everyone course presents a model program for community preparedness. In addition, resources materials are available to help organizations conduct simple preparedness activities for everyone.

Course Summary

Congratulations! You have completed this course and now should understand the critical leadership role you play in an emergency management program. You can continue the learning process by completing the following steps:

- Step 1: Understand the Emergency Management Mission
- Step 2: Review Your Authorities
- Step 3: Learn About Your Team
- Step 4: Review Your Plans and Resources
- Step 5: Know How To Lead During a Crisis
- Step 6: Promote Community Preparedness